# The Camp System

**Jane Shuter**

Heinemann LIBRARY

# www.heinemann.co.uk/library

Visit our website to find out more information about **Heinemann Library** books.

To order:
- ☎ Phone 44 (0) 1865 888066
- 🖹 Send a fax to 44 (0) 1865 314091
- 💻 Visit the Heinemann Bookshop at www.heinemann.co.uk/library to browse our catalogue and order online.

First published in Great Britain by Heinemann Library, Halley Court, Jordan Hill, Oxford OX2 8EJ, part of Harcourt Education. Heinemann is a registered trademark of Harcourt Education Ltd.

© Harcourt Education Ltd 2002
The moral right of the proprietor has been asserted.

Editorial: Andrew Farrow and Georga Godwin
Design: Joanna Sapwell and Tinstar Design (www.tinstar.co.uk)
Illustrations: Martin Griffin
Picture Research: Maria Joannou and Thelma Gilbert
Production: Viv Hichens

Originated by Ambassador Litho Ltd
Printed in Hong Kong by Wing King Tong

ISBN 0 431 15361 2
06 05 04 03 02
10 9 8 7 6 5 4 3 2 1

**British Library Cataloguing in Publication Data**
Shuter, Jane
The Holocaust: The Camp System
940.5'318
A full catalogue record for this book is available from the British Library.

**Acknowledgements**
The Publishers would like to thank the following for permission to reproduce photographs: AKG pp. **4**, **13**, **26**, **42**; Auschwitz Museum pp. **22**, **31**, **33**, **40**; Auschwitz-Birkenau State Museum pp. **16**, **25**, **27**, **36**, **43**, **44**; BPK p. **20**; Corbis p. **17**; Emma Robertson p. **39**; Emma Robertson & Magnet Harlequin pp. **24**, **24**, **28**, **32**, **34**, **37**, **45**; Mary Evans Picture Library p. **29**; Popperfoto p. **5**; The Good Old Days p. **19**; Tomi Ungerer & Diogene Verlag AG Zurich pp. **14**, **18**; Ullstein Bild p. **35**; Ullstein Bilder Dienst p. **15**; USHMM pp. **9**, **10**, **11**, **12**, **38**, **46**, **47**, **49**; Weimar Picture Library p. **6**; Yad Vashem p. **7**.

Cover photograph shows camp records of prisoners at Auschwitz, reproduced with permission of USHMM.

The publishers would like to thank Jonathan Gorsky of the Council of Christians and Jews for his assistance in the preparation of this book.

Every effort has been made to contact copyright holders of any material reproduced in this book. Any omissions will be rectified in subsequent printings if notice is given to the publishers.

# Contents

Words appearing in the text in bold, **like this**, are explained in the Glossary.

# Camps and the Holocaust

When the **Nazi** Party, led by Adolf Hitler, came to power in Germany in 1933, it wanted to set up the perfect Nazi state. The Nazis wanted to stamp out any opposition to their rule, so they set up a system of camps for holding people they saw as '**undesirable**'. The Nazis said the camps would re-educate prisoners to accept Nazi ideas. Camps were different from ordinary prisons because the prisoners had not been convicted of any crime and there was no date set for their release.

The early camps were concentration camps for **political** opponents. The first of these, Dachau, was set up just a few days after the Nazis won the March 1933 election.

The camps were run by the **SS** (short for *Schutzstaffel* – security staff). The SS had been set up as Hitler's private bodyguard, and they all swore an oath of loyalty to Hitler, not Germany. Led by Heinrich Himmler, the SS eventually grew to take over parts of the German army.

## Early prisoners

Some of the earliest prisoners in Dachau concentration camp were political opponents of the Nazis, mostly **Communists** and **Social Democrats**, just like the prisoners in this photograph.

Some were **Jewish**, but they were there for their political beliefs not what the Nazis saw as their **race**. The camp was built to hold 5000 people. The rules read to prisoners arriving in Dachau began:

'Tolerance means weakness. Punishment will be mercilessly handed out whenever Germany's interests make it necessary. A person who is decent but misled will never be affected by these punishment regulations. But political stirrers be warned: watch out that you are not caught, for you will be hung.'

## Different prisoners

The Nazis changed from only putting political opponents in camps to using camps to imprison all kinds of people that they did not want in their perfect state. Among these were Jews. Jewish people see themselves as a people with common ancestors that stretch back to Biblical times. Jews are united by their religion, Judaism, and by a strong culture. The Nazis also called people Jews if they had Jewish ancestors, even if they had changed their faith. The Nazis moved from imprisoning Jews to killing all Jews in German-controlled lands. This mass murder of about 5.7 million Jews, and other so-called undesirables, is called the **Holocaust**. The camps were vital in making the Holocaust happen.

## How were ghettos different from camps?

**Ghettos** were areas of towns walled off from the rest of the town where Jews were forced to live. They were crowded, but families could live together and follow their religion. In a camp, families were split up. All prisoners followed prison routine, from waking to going to sleep. There were regular **roll calls** when guards checked that everyone was there. Camp prisoners ate only camp food and did the work the guards gave them. They could not follow their religion. This book only looks at the camps and the way they were run. Another book in this series, *Life and Death in Hitler's Europe*, looks more closely at life in the ghettos.

**How do we know?**

- One of the most important sources of information are survivors of the camps. Some told their memories directly – other wrote stories and poems or painted and drew the camps.
- Official Nazi documents show what went on in the camps, although the Germans did try to destroy the evidence.
- A few camps still stand, such as Dachau and Auschwitz-Birkenau.
- The Nuremberg Trials of 1945-6, held after the defeat of Germany in the Second World War, used descriptions of what went on in the camps.
- Some people who did not survive hid writings or pictures, which were later found.
- The soldiers who **liberated** the camps recorded what they saw in words, on film and in pictures.

# Types of camp

There were three main types of camp: concentration camps, labour camps and death camps. They were the same in that:

- They were fenced off from the outside world, guarded and run by soldiers.
- They gave prisoners the bare minimum of food and shelter.
- Prisoners were imprisoned there without trial and were given no date for their release. They were badly treated and harshly punished.
- The biggest camps had at least one **crematorium**, for burning the bodies of the hundreds of prisoners who died. The fact that crematoria were built from the start shows that prisoners were expected to die in large numbers in the camps.

## Concentration camps

Concentration camps were set up from 1933, as soon as the **Nazis** came to power. They were used to imprison all kinds of people that the Nazis labelled **undesirable**, from political opponents to **Jehovah's Witnesses**. Many were **Jewish**. The Nazis said these prisoners were in **protective custody** because they were a threat to Germany. They said prisoners would be re-educated to accept Nazi beliefs and then released. This sometimes happened. However, more prisoners died in the camps than were released. There were 30,000 deaths recorded in Dachau camp between 1933 and 1945. Many thousands more deaths were unrecorded. And this was a camp built to re-educate people, not kill them.

## New types of prisoners

By 1935 the Nazis had crushed most political opposition, so fewer '**politicals**' were sent to concentration camps. The Nazis discussed shutting down the camps, but instead they decided to send different people there. They used the camps to shut up '**asocials**' and people from **races** they thought of as inferior. The Nazis had very strong, but wrong ideas about race. They invented a pure **Aryan** race for themselves – white, blonde-haired, blue-eyed and healthy, such as the ideal family shown in this poster. The Nazis invented other races, such as Slavs (for instance Poles and people from the Soviet Union) and Jews that they saw as sub-human and inferior. The number of prisoners kept rising, despite the terrible death rates.

## Labour camps

Labour camps were built near factories or workplaces, such as stone quarries, so the prisoners would act as cheap labour, like the Plaszow camp pictured here. However, even here, work was not the most important aim. From the start, the Nazis spoke about *Vernichtung durch Arbeit* – destruction through work – when talking about labour camps. People did work, but their living and working conditions were awful, so they did not work well. A doctor who visited the labour camps in Poland in 1940 reported to the **SS**:

'The rooms are totally unsuitable. They are dark and dirty and full of fleas and lice. There are 75 people in a room 5 metres by 6 metres: sleeping on the floor, without straw, lying on top of each other. The roofs leak, the windows have no glass. Three out of every ten workers have no shoes, trousers or shirts. There is no soap or water and the sick are crammed in with the healthy.'

## Death camps

Death camps were set up in 1941, to kill as many Jewish people as possible, as efficiently as possible. Millions of Jews were already being killed in concentration camps and labour camps. They died from starvation, disease and exhaustion. They were also worked to death, beaten to death and executed for various 'crimes'. However, death camps were different. They had specially designed **gas chambers** for mass killing. There were four main death camps: Chelmno, Belzec, Sobibor and Treblinka. Death camps could unload and kill each **transport** of Jews within two hours. The camps had few barracks or other buildings – they were not needed. Most people sent to death camps were killed straight away. They did not work, eat or sleep there. Only a few hundred 'work Jews' were left alive to clean out the ovens, bury the ashes of the dead and sort out and send off their possessions. The official Polish estimates are that at least 2 million Jews and about 52,000 gypsies were killed in just these four camps between December 1941 and October 1943. That is over 20,000 people killed each day, seven days a week. Death camps were also added to the existing camps of Auschwitz and Majdanek, but these camps still provided workers, so had barracks, showers and other buildings.

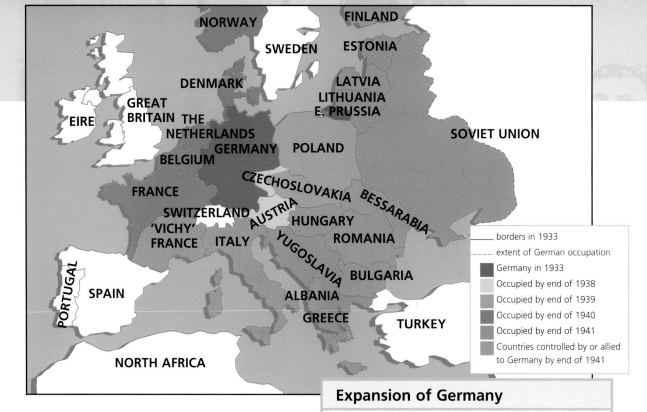

borders in 1933
- - - extent of German occupation
Germany in 1933
Occupied by end of 1938
Occupied by end of 1939
Occupied by end of 1940
Occupied by end of 1941
Countries controlled by or allied to Germany by end of 1941

## Expansion of Germany

This map shows the land taken over by Germany between 1933 and 1941.

## Marching across Europe

Hitler and the Nazis used the German army to take over more and more land in Europe. The Nazis wanted to set up a new German Europe, a Greater Germany or **Third Reich**. When the Nazis invaded Poland, Britain and France declared war on Germany on 3 September 1939, hoping to stop the expansion. The Second World War had begun.

## More camps

As the war went on, the camp system grew rapidly and became more complicated. Different sorts of camps were set up to cope with new kinds of prisoners and the demands that war made on people and factories. Some camps contained several types of camp within the main camp.

- Prisoner-of-war camps: as soon as Germany was at war its army began to take prisoners from the armies it was fighting. The soldiers were supposed to be put in prisoner-of-war camps and treated according to the Geneva Convention – a set of rules written to make sure that soldiers from the other side are treated fairly. French and British soldiers were mostly treated well, although some were used as workers. When the USA joined the war their soldiers were treated fairly, too. Russian prisoners of war, however, were more likely to be sent to concentration camps, starved or killed because Nazi ideas about race classified them as Slavs.

- Transit camps: as the war progressed, Germany steadily took control of more and more of Europe. Jews and other non-Aryans in occupied lands were sent to the camps. The Nazis set up transit camps in occupied countries like France, Holland and Belgium. Millions of people, mostly Jewish, were held for a short time in transit camps until they could be taken to camps in Poland, which had been made into part of Greater Germany.

- Sub-camps: as concentration camps and labour camps grew, smaller camps, often some way away from the main camp, were set up. These sub-camps were often near a particular factory or farmland, so the prisoners could be used as labour. Sub-camps had high death rates too, so brought in replacement prisoners from the main camps.

## Changing camps to help the war

By 1941, the German government had made so many men join the army that it was desperate for workers in factories, especially in those making war goods. So camp prisoners did more and more of the war work.

The Inspector of Concentration Camps from 1940, Richard Glücks, wrote in 1942: 'All the camps are asking for prisoners, since they do not have enough to meet the demands for labour. All camp commanders must make sure everyone who can work is doing so.'

Conditions in some camps changed to get the best out of their workers. Oswald Pohl, responsible for organizing the work wrote to all concentration camp **commandants** on 15 May 1943:

'The extent and urgency of the work carried out by prisoners needs every prisoner working to the highest standard. Present results must be improved. Prisoners who work hard and behave well will be granted privileges, including more freedom of movement; extra food; money; tobacco; permission to grow their hair.'

### Auschwitz

Auschwitz was the most complicated of all the camps. It had a concentration camp (Auschwitz I), a labour camp (Buna/Monowice) and a death camp (Auschwitz-Birkenau). It also had about 40 sub-camps attached to the labour camp. Finally, it had prisoner-of-war camps, close to the factories. This photo, taken by the British from the air in June 1944, shows Auschwitz I (bottom) and Auschwitz-Birkenau (top).

AUSCHWITZ-BIRKENAU COMPLEX
OSWIECIM, POLAND
26 JUNE 1944

# Prisoners

There were many different kinds of prisoners in the camps. Both the prisoners and guards in all the camps made clear distinctions between different sorts of prisoners. The camps quickly developed a fixed 'power structure'.

## Positions of power

German criminals were most likely to be made **prisoner functionaries**. This meant they were put in charge of other prisoners as *kapos* (in charge of work) or *blockältesters* (in charge of the barracks). The **SS** chose criminals with a violent past, who were more likely to enjoy, or at least not object to, the violence they were expected to hand out to the other prisoners. Rudolph Hoess, the first **commandant** of Auschwitz, said of German criminals: 'Almost without exception they had "high" positions and so were given all the physical necessities of life.'

## In the middle

**Politicals** were in the middle of the prisoner hierarchy. They were above **asocials** – anyone who did not fit in, from homosexuals to alcoholics. People in these two groups might be given a 'soft' (easy) job, like working in the camp kitchens. Prisoners who did indoor work were likely to live longer than those who worked outdoors, or in the factories. German or German-speaking politicals sometimes worked in the offices, or listed the prisoners arriving at camp. The **Nazis** did not value intellectuals (anyone with more than a basic education) very highly, as they may disagree with Nazi ideals. Even so, the Nazis saw that intellectuals were useful for office work – record keeping was a vital part of keeping the camp system running.

## Classifying prisoners

Each prisoner was given a number and a coloured triangle to sew on to their uniform when they arrived at a camp. These were handed out according to the Nazi classification of prisoners shown on the official Nazi chart opposite. Professional criminals had green triangles. Political prisoners and Christian priests had red. Asocials wore black triangles, and gypsies wore brown. **Jehovah's Witnesses** wore violet triangles and homosexuals, pink. **Jews** were put into one of the above groups, then given an extra yellow triangle to show they were Jews.

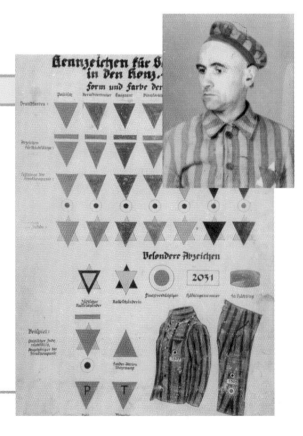

## The sick

Sick people were always treated badly, no matter what their camp classification. If they could not work, they were of no use. Anyone who became ill tried to hide their sickness for as long as possible. Sick prisoners were sent to the hospital. Here they got little or no medical attention or food. They were left alone to die or get better. Sometimes they were chosen for medical experiments. The person in this photo was used for experiments looking into surviving at high altitudes. He is still wearing the harness used in the experiment.

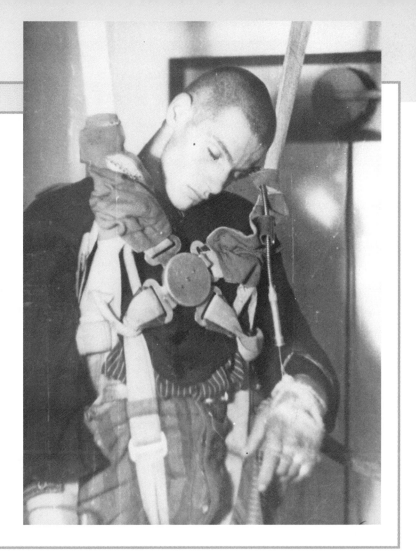

## The lowest of the low

Poles, Russians, gypsies and Jews – in that order – had to do the worst jobs and had the worst living conditions and food. This is because the Nazis saw them as separate, inferior **races**. The yellow triangle worn by Jewish people marked them out for special treatment. The **SS** who ran the camps made it clear to the prisoners in charge that they could treat Jews more brutally than anyone else. Many *kapos* were Germans who believed Nazi **propaganda** about inferior races, so were happy to mistreat Jews.

## Special cases

Any prisoner who annoyed one of the SS could be killed – even a *kapo*. If a prisoner appeared for **roll call** 'improperly dressed' they could be shot, or just be punished.

Most camps had Penal Companies – punishment units where prisoners were kept in specially guarded barracks. Very few people survived being sent to the punishment units. Prisoners were sent there for so-called crimes, such as smoking a cigarette at work or wearing more clothes than they had been given.

# How camps were used

The camps were used in several different ways. They are mostly known for their part in the **Holocaust**, but the first camps were used to imprison the **Nazis' political** opponents, or people that the Nazis saw as opponents. The early camps were also used to imprison **asocials** – anyone the Nazis said were not supporting the Nazi state. The difference between the camps and ordinary prisons was that people were sent to the camps without trial and without a date for release. So, how did the Nazis justify setting up these camps?

## Public safety

The Nazis said they set up concentration camps 'to keep Germany safe'. Why? On 28 February 1933 the Reichstag, the German parliament, was set on fire. The Nazis produced a young **Communist** who confessed to starting the fire. The next day Hitler persuaded President Von Hindenburg to pass an emergency decree 'for the Protection of the People and State'. This let the **Gestapo** take people into **protective custody** if they might be a danger to Germany. They did not have the right to a trial, nor a date for release. The Nazis used the law to arrest political opponents, or anyone they felt like arresting, and send them to concentration camps.

## Hard work

The Nazis said that the concentration camps were to re-educate their opponents and asocials. Drunks, tramps, beggars and the unemployed are typical examples of people the Nazis called asocial. Nazi **propaganda** said that if all these people went to the camps, through hard work and prison routine, they would come to see that Nazi ideas were right. Hard physical work was seen as good for everyone at the time. As soon as they came to power in 1933, the Nazis set up labour service camps where all young men and women at university had to do 'labour service'. The Nazis said that working hard was a duty that **citizens** owed to Germany. People who did not work were letting the country down.

## Release certificate

In the early days of the camps some prisoners were released. This photo shows Fritz Echer's release certificate from Dachau camp on 29 January 1934. Released prisoners were closely watched at first. They had to register with the police in the place they went to live and report to the police station weekly, or even daily. If they seemed to be behaving themselves they had to report less and less often.

### Re-education

The Nazis said that concentration camp prisoners also needed to be rescued from wrong ideas that they might have been infected with. Werner Schaefer, the **commandant** of Oranienburg concentration camp, said: 'One should not underestimate the difficulty and value of such educational work. The character of many German people has been damaged by fourteen years of poverty, unemployment and lack of clear leadership.' He wrote a book about re-education in the camps in 1934, in which he said many of the prisoners had thanked him, with tears in their eyes, as they left; several had offered to pay for similar re-education for their sons.

### A genuine danger?

At first, the Gestapo arrested genuine political opponents. As time passed, the Gestapo arrested people for less and less reason. Bernt Engelmann, a young man in Hitler's Germany, later a journalist, remembers:

> 'When I was arrested and sent to Anrath prison, I saw the other prisoners only during our daily 'walk', fifteen minutes of shuffling round in a circle in a courtyard. We were forbidden to speak, but of course we whispered to each other.

> 'The man in the cell next to mine, Marinus, a welder from Rotterdam, had been walking his dog one evening. A German patrol came by, and the dog barked at them. They shot the dog and took Marinus with them there and then. His family had no idea what had happened to him.'

In 1938 an officer from the part of the **SS** that collected information and spied on people, reported with satisfaction that he had many useful informers:

> 'In a café a 64-year-old woman said to the person she was sitting with: "Mussolini has more political sense in one of his boots than Hitler has in his brain." Other customers overheard the remark and one made a phone call. Five minutes later she was arrested by the Gestapo.'

13

### The value of work

Was the work done in the camps valuable? The Nazis argued that it was. There were various kinds of work that was useful to the **Third Reich** – Hitler's new German empire. It was the prisoners who built the camps and kept them running. They kept the camp buildings and roads repaired and extended the camps so more prisoners could be accommodated. They did the cooking and cleaning and made the clothes and furniture. This kept the running costs of the camps as low as possible, so they were not a burden on the state. The camps also kept the prisoners away from ordinary people.

### Cheap workers

Prisoners worked for the Nazis directly in stone quarries, in workshops in the camp and in state factories. The SS ran several profitable businesses using camp labour. Camp prisoners also farmed nearby land but most of the food they grew went to the nearest towns, not to the camp kitchens. The profits went to the SS.

### Winter Aid

Prisoners in some camps made a variety of small books and toys for children. These were sold in the street for the *Winterhilfswerk* (Winter Aid), a charity that helped 'deserving' poor Germans. Everybody was expected to take their turn doing the selling, as Paul Kremer, a doctor at Auschwitz, noted in his diary: '2 March 1944: today the local Party group told me I had to collect again. I had to sell 100 tiny china badges of characters from fairy stories.'

## Building works

Albert Speer was an architect who designed buildings for Hitler. Speer designed the new Olympic Stadium, shown here. He planned new towns in Germany and estimated he would need 2 billion bricks just for his building work in Berlin in 1938. The German brickyards could only make 350 million bricks. To avoid buying bricks from abroad, Himmler created new camps like Buchenwald and Sachsenhausen, to make the bricks that were needed. These camps were built near rock quarries or clay pits for this purpose.

## Cheap labour

Some camp prisoners worked for local businesses, which paid the SS. The fee varied over the years but was always low. In 1944, the SS worked out it cost 1.34 **Reichmarks (RM)** to keep each male prisoner and 1.22 RM for each woman per day. They were charging businesses 4 to 6 marks a day for their workers – Auschwitz made 15-20 billion RM from hiring out their prisoners in 1944.

## War work

From 1939, when Germany was at war, the Nazis needed workers to replace those called into the army and those making war goods.

In April 1942 Oswald Pohl, who was in charge of organizing war work for the camps, wrote: 'War means the camp structure and work of the prisoners need to be changed. Work is more important than re-education. This will affect the way the camps are run.' On the same day he told each camp commandant:

> 'Camp commandants are responsible for maximum productivity. They must set work hours, which must be exhausting – full production must be met. There are no limits to the hours of work. Things that shorten working time (meals, roll calls, etc.) are to be kept to a minimum. Long marches to and from the camps for meals are banned.'

Pohl also set up a system of rewards for hard working prisoners. The improved conditions did not apply to **Jewish** people.

## Medical experiments

The Nazis used camp prisoners for medical experiments. They saw this as another way the camps could be useful. Experiments did not go on in every camp. It depended on the size of the camp and the interests of the camp doctors. Medical experiments were carried out for three official reasons: to help the army, to help Germany after the war and to try to prove the racial ideas invented by the Nazis. Camps also tested new drugs for various German firms.

In one set of experiments, prisoners were given **frostbite** by exposing them, naked, to freezing conditions. The frostbite was allowed to develop into gangrene – a deadly infection if untreated. Doctors then experimented to find the best treatments for frostbite and gangrene, which affected many German soldiers fighting the **Allies**.

SS doctors also used camp patients to teach nurses how to perform operations. After practising on patients, whose deaths did not matter to the Nazis, they could operate and save the lives of German soldiers.

Experiments were also carried out on common camp diseases, like **typhus** and various fevers. In Mauthausen, Dr Karl Gross injected patients with typhus and **cholera** germs to test various new vaccines. Paul Kremer, a doctor at Auschwitz, arrived in the camp on 30 August 1943: 'Arrived to find camp in **quarantine** – malaria, typhus and dysentery are raging.' There was still typhus a month later. Kremer also collected lice, which spread the diseases, from the patients for vaccine experiments.

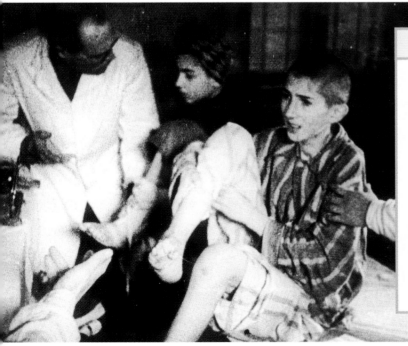

### Not an experiment

While some patients were forced into conditions where they got frostbite as a medical experiment, many more got it as a result of the dreadful living and working conditions. This photo shows patients with frostbite, being treated by Red Cross doctors once Auschwitz camp was **liberated**. Many patients, in all the camps, were terrified of doctors and hospitals after their years in the camps and did not want the Red Cross doctors to treat them.

## A healthy race

Hitler saw children as the future. He believed they would love and obey him in a country full of fit, racially pure Aryans. This view of the future meant there was no room in Germany for the sick, the disabled or those believed by the Nazis to be **racially inferior**. Many medical experiments in the camps aimed at finding ways to get rid of so-called racially inferior people. Hitler loved to have his photo taken with beautiful, healthy children. Here he is posing with members of the Hitler Youth.

## A better Germany?

Another set of experiments was intended to work out a way to stop 'unfit' people from having children – to sterilize them. To the Nazis, unfit people included non-**Aryans** and physically and mentally disabled people. The Nazis wanted to find a quicker, cheaper way to sterilize people than by operations on each person, which took too long and cost too much. They used X-rays and chemical injections. Only a few of the prisoners survived.

A different programme fed about 100,000 prisoners in Mauthausen, Sachsenhausen, Buchenwald and Dachau camps a new meatless sausage, which, if safe, would be a cheap food for Germans after the war. All versions of the sausage caused bad stomach upsets and damage to the digestive system, some of it permanent. The idea was abandoned.

## Racial ideas

Some SS doctors collected skeletons and various body parts, such as the brain, to prove their ideas about **race**. They wanted to show that Aryans, the race that they invented for themselves, was definitely a race and that as Aryans they were better than other races – with stronger skeletons and organs, bigger brains and so on. Prisoners of certain races defined by the Nazis were chosen from those in the camps and measured and tested. They were then killed. The bodies that supported Nazi ideas about race were sent to Hitler. He had a collection of skeletons that he planned to use after the war to teach Nazi racial ideas.

## Judenfrei

The Nazis had a final use for the camps. They did not openly explain this use, although the SS and the camp prisoners were well aware of it. The camps were to help make the lands controlled by Germany **Judenfrei** – Jew Free. In the early 1930s, some prisoners, including Jews, were released from the camps. This was when Jews were being encouraged to emigrate. The Nazis felt that some experience of being in the camps would help Jews to decide to leave Germany. Those who did not emigrate were rounded up at regular intervals and shut in the camps or in specially created **ghettos**.

## Murder in the camps

In the camps, Jewish people had the worst living and working conditions. Hundred of them died in the camps every day, from overwork, starvation and disease. Yet more died from brutal beatings or harsh punishments given out by the SS guards. Others were executed – hung or shot for crimes such as holding secret meetings or refusing to obey an order. They were also labelled mentally ill and sent to clinics, where they were killed. Franz Ziereis, commandant of Mauthausen, said: 'About 20,000 prisoners, including real mentally handicapped ones, were sent to Hartseim Institute and gassed.' Of course, other prisoners also died in the camps – but the death rates of Jews, Poles and Slavs were the highest.

## Papers and passes

Every time the German army took more land, it took over more Jewish people as part of the new population. Each time, it set up anti-Jewish measures. The people of each newly occupied country found they needed a lot of passes and documents just to go about their daily lives. They also needed papers proving that they were not Jewish, to stop them from being sent to the camps. For example, this certificate and pass book state that the Ungerer family in Alsace are pure Aryans, not Jewish.

## Hiding the evidence

When the Nazis saw that they were losing the war they tried to cover up what had happened in the camps. In some cases, as at Auschwitz, they left it too late to destroy everything. The camp, and evidence that shows what had happened there, survived. At Treblinka, however, they shut the camp down after it was set alight in a prisoner revolt, in August 1943. This gave the Nazis time to build the farmhouse pictured here on the site to pretend that there had never been a camp at all.

## Death camps

In 1941, Hans Frank, governor of Nazi-occupied Poland, said: 'We must exterminate the Jews wherever and whenever we find them, in order to maintain Reich control here.' Then in January 1942, the Nazis had a meeting in Wannsee, near Berlin, to discuss what they saw as the 'Jewish Problem'. This was the first time mass murder was openly discussed as the 'Final Solution'.

At the meeting, Nazi leaders agreed that emigration had failed – they would not succeed in removing Jews using 'legal' means. So they decided that Jews must be sent east and kept in labour camps. In these camps 'a large number will drop out through natural wastage.' Those who survive 'will have to be dealt with accordingly.' What the Nazis meant by this was that the Jews would be killed, as efficiently as possible.

A new type of camp, the death camp, was set up at Belzec, Chelmno, Sobibor and Treblinka. Auschwitz and Madjanek each had a death camp added.

Kurt Gerstein, an SS officer, watched one gassing at Belzec:

'The train arrives, 45 wagons with about 6700 people, about 1450 of them dead on arrival. They leave their baggage, undress, have their heads shaved, then go into the death chambers. An officer tells them: "Nothing is going to happen to you. Breath in deeply, the gas is needed to strengthen you, because of all the sickness and epidemics." They pack them in 700-800 to a chamber. The engine finally starts and after 32 minutes they are all dead.'

**19**

# Running the camps

The camps were run by the **SS**. The leader of the SS, Heinrich Himmler, also ran the **Gestapo** – the secret police. Himmler was one of the first **Nazi** Party members, and a friend of Hitler's. He divided up the SS and made different people responsible for each part, but they did not always work well together.

Himmler's Inspector of Concentration Camps from 1934 to 1940 was Theodore Eicke, who made it clear to the guards that they should have no pity for any enemy of the state – that is, any concentration camp prisoner. He told all camp commanders: 'It is the duty of every SS man to identify himself, body and soul, with the cause. Every order must be carried out, even the most difficult of them, without hesitation.' The camps eventually needed a huge number of SS to run them – 6000 at Auschwitz alone.

## Day-to-day control

The SS who worked as guards controlled the daily routine of the camps, organized the prisoners or worked in the offices. Any SS man could punish a prisoner, but the clerks who organized the prisoners' food, transport and work could cut themselves off from what went on. The SS men in charge of the prisoners had the most opportunities to treat them badly, and the least chance of pretending they didn't know what was going on. They held **roll calls** that lasted several hours, despite blazing heat, pouring rain or freezing snow. They inspected barracks and prisoners, handing out punishments if everything wasn't perfect. Prisoners were beaten and humiliated. They could be shot for anything or nothing.

## Gas vans in Chelmno

Not all the bad jobs were given to prisoners. For example, low-ranking SS men drove the gas vans at Chelmno. One of them, Walter Burmeister, said at his trial after the war:

> 'When the lorries were full the double doors at the back were closed and the exhaust fitted to the inside of the van. I started the engine and let it run until the people inside had suffocated. Then I drove to the burial place. When I got back the van was cleaned out for the next run. I can no longer say what I thought at the time.'

One SS guard, questioned after the war, said that it was possible to ask not to take part in the brutality:

> 'You had to make it sound like a request, due to your weakness, not refusing an order (which would get you shot). If you did this you usually ended up at a desk, where you could ignore what was going on. Of course, it didn't help your career – you didn't get promotion that way.'

## The Hierarchy of the *SS*

**Führer**
**(Adolf Hitler)**

*Reichsführer der SS* (Heinrich Himmler)

**Inspector for**
**Concentration Camps**

**Head of**
**Economic Enterprises**

**Camp Commandant**

| **Political Office** | **Commandant's Office** | **Camp Administration** | **Economic Administration** | **SS Hospital** |
|---|---|---|---|---|
| Arranged reception, processing, discharge of prisoners. Kept prisoners' records. Also administered death certificates, etc. Ran crematoria, investigated crimes, ran spy systems. | Organized all the SS staff. | Dealt with the prisoners, including punishments, food, housing, roll calls, executions. | Bought and sold all supplies to and from the outside world. | Care for the SS. Experiments on the prisoners. |

**SS Officers**

**SS Soldiers**

'prisoner functionaries' (*see page 24*)

## Women

The SS used mainly women officers to run the women's camps. However, women could only go so far in the SS. They were not allowed to be in charge of male camps, or even large women's camps. They ran the smaller women's camps and had female **kapos**. The SS guards were still men. Johanna Langefeldt became head of the Women's Camp at Auschwitz-Birkenau, under Rudolf Hoess, the **commandant** of all the Auschwitz camps. Hoess disapproved of Langefeldt and of her *kapos*, who he said: 'were worse than the men in their toughness, vindictiveness and depravity. Some were truly repulsive creatures.'

## Who was involved?

Himmler, Eicke and Pohl were based in offices in Berlin. They were not involved in the brutality of the camps on a daily basis. Even the camp commandants, who lived in their camps, could choose not to be involved in the day-to-day brutality of camp life. After the war, Rudolf Hoess, the commandant of Auschwitz, suggested that camp commandants were not really the ones who ran the camps:

> 'I wanted to get useful work out of the prisoners, so wanted to give them better treatment than was usual in concentration camps. But my efforts to do this were in vain, because the officers ran the camp in the Eicke way. The real ruler of every concentration camp is not the camp commander, but the officer in charge of the camp. It was this officer who taught his men how to behave, and it was they who taught the *kapos*, from the chief block leader down to the last block clerk, how to behave.'

This was, clearly, an attempt to excuse his involvement in the **Holocaust**.

## Careful choice of words

Most Nazis used words like 'filth' and 'vermin' to make **Jews** seem less like people. They also used words to cover up acts of cruelty and mass murder. They used these words in documents to hide what they were doing. But they also used them in conversation – as a way of not looking clearly at what was going on. They used the terms 'special treatment' and 'disinfection' to refer to killing prisoners. They said prisoners were on 'work detail', when really they were being given pointless, dangerous jobs to do to work them to death. 'Special actions' were mass gassings or mass shootings. 'Natural wastage' meant prisoners dying through the terrible camp conditions. However, not everyone was always so careful. Karl Jager, head of ***Einsatzkommando*** 3, an SS death squad sent into Russia behind the invading German army to murder Jews, reported in December 1941: 'I now want to bump off the "work Jews" and their families – all that remain in my area.'

One of the SS guards at Treblinka death camp had a St Bernard dog called Barry that he taught to attack Jewish prisoners when he gave the order: 'Man, bite the dog!'. Another guard said at his trial: 'By "man" he meant the dog, Barry, and by "dog" he meant the prisoners.' He did not try to hide his contempt for Jewish people. He went out of his way to make things even more unbearable for them.

## Working in the camps

The head of the Economic and Administrative Office, Oswald Pohl, had to make sure the camps made a profit. In 1938 he set up the first SS-controlled company, the German Earth & Stone Works. More SS companies, like this one painted by a survivor, were set up, all making a good profit. Pohl also hired out workers to German companies. Pohl wanted prisoners who were fit to work and worked well. This clashed with Eicke's system of brutal punishments and bad working and living conditions. Yves Beon, a French prisoner in the Dora camp, remembered:

'Since 13 March 1944, the death rate has been high, with no incoming people. The population is dropping, yet the work must increase. The SS believe the perfect cure for the drop in numbers is – more beatings! With a good club, miracles can be worked, as long as an expert is using it.'

## Prisoner functionaries

The SS used prisoners to do the day-to-day organizing of other prisoners. These **prisoner functionaries** lived longer. Some filled in forms or organized the kitchen stores. But most prisoner functionaries had to make other prisoners do something – often by beating them. The SS gave these jobs to 'green' prisoners, that is prisoners who wore a green triangle on their uniforms to show they were in prison for committing a crime, not for political or racial reasons. Green prisoners were mainly German criminals who did not mind the violence, and who even shared the Nazis' hatred of Jews, Poles and Slavs and were happy to beat them up. But they were still prisoners and life for them was not safe. The SS gave them power, but could take it away at any time. As a prisoner from

Dora said: 'They had armbands and warm clothes and boots, but they knew they would die, too, one way or another. Even after eight years they still had fear eating away at them.'

*Kapos* were prisoners who were put in charge of other prisoners. In most camps, the *kapos* were organized by a *lagerältester* – a camp leader. A prisoner from Mauthausen later explained the system:

'The SS *Kommandoführer* [leader of a work squad] told the SS men under him what work their part of the squad had to do each day. The SS then told the *kapos* what they wanted done. Each *kapo*, or one of his *hilfskapo* [assistant *kapo*], "encouraged" a prisoner to do his job with bull whips, rubber clubs, rods and so on.'

**24**

### Blockältesters

Each barrack had a *blockältester* who had to get everyone up on time and ready for roll call. They made sure the prisoners kept themselves and their barracks as clean as possible and gave out the food. In return, depending on the size of the camp, each *blockältester* had his own room, or at least his own bed. Hugo Gryn, sent to Auschwitz as a teenager, remembers his first meeting with a *blockältester*:

'He was a fairly young man with an armband marked "*Blockälteste 7*". He had two assistants and the three of them lined us up in "proper order", as they called it. There were about 700 of us and by the time we had "learned" how to line up, dismiss, and line up again, we were exhausted and very hungry.'

The *blockältester* and his assistants went and fetched the food. The prisoners were each given a small piece of bread with a spoonful of jam on it and told that had to last 24 hours.

### Administration

Prisoners also worked in the administration buildings, filling in forms and typing out orders or reports. Sometimes they had more difficult work. Tadeusz Sobolewicz, a Polish prisoner who spoke German, had to register Jews who were not sent straight to their deaths in the **gas chambers** at Auschwitz-Birkenau.

'I had to write almost without pause. "Where and when were you born? Name? Where do you want your letters sent?" It was hard work and I knew it wasn't needed, any of this information. From time to time I would look one of them in the eye – did they know? That night I couldn't sleep. I could see the red glow in the sky where they were burning the relatives of the people I had processed.'

This photo, taken by the SS, shows prisoners like Tadeusz Sobolewicz waiting to process new arrivals to Auschwitz.

## The worst work

Death camps, like Auschwitz-Birkenau, used *kapos* in **selection** – deciding who would live and who would die as people climbed off the trains. On 11 August 1942 about 1000 men women and children arrived in Auschwitz-Birkenau from Sosnowitz **Ghetto**. Only 46 men were chosen to live. SS men did the choosing, but the *kapos* got people into line, forced families apart, unloaded the baggage and took it to be sorted. As part of the unloading process they had to drag out dead bodies, and search the filthy wagons for valuables. Then they had to clean both the wagons and the platform.

## A helping hand

Some *kapos* were able to help prisoners. They knew what was going to happen to new arrivals. In Auschwitz-Birkenau some new arrivals were sent straight to their deaths, while others were kept alive for a while as workers. *Kapos* knew how those who were selected for work were chosen. So they could sometimes help someone survive. This was a big risk – if they were caught doing this they would have been shot or sent to the gas chambers. Hugo Gryn remembers how a *kapo* saved his life:

'The men in striped trousers took away the luggage. I didn't want to give up my rucksack. The man who took it away from me said something in Polish. I replied in German that I did not understand. "You are nineteen and you are a mechanic, or something like it! Don't forget, nineteen!" As he said this to me, he kept looking sideways in case he was seen talking.'

Hugo told his father who said he should do as the man said. Hugo was selected for work.

### Selection

This photo of selection in Auschwitz-Birkenau, taken by the SS, shows the early stages in the selection process for a transport of Jewish people from Hungary in 1944. You can see an SS officer (in the peaked cap), an SS guard (behind the officer) and the *kapos* (in the striped uniforms) waiting to empty the train.

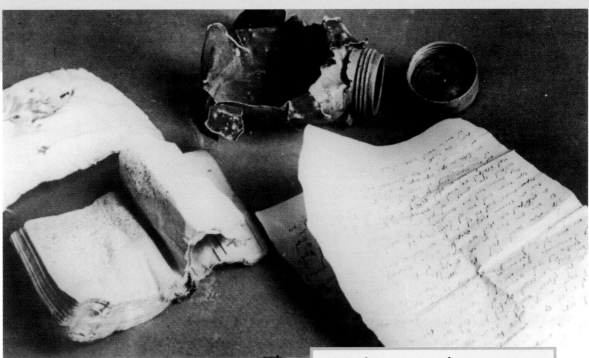

## Sonderkommando

The *Sonderkommando* (Special Detachment) were Jewish men who were forced to take people to the gas chambers, remove the corpses from the gas chambers and burn them in the **crematoria** ovens. Anyone refusing to do this work was sent straight to the gas chambers with the next transport. The *Sonderkommando* did not take part in the gassing itself. Rudolf Hoess, commandant at Auschwitz, explained that it was important to have *Sonderkommando* prisoners there: 'The calm behaviour of the Special Detachment reassured those who were worried or suspicious about what was going on. They might not believe the SS, but they would believe one of their own **race**.' Hoess said that the *Sonderkommando* co-operated in creating calm: 'They lied to the new arrivals very convincingly. I never heard of any of them telling, or even hinting, of what lay ahead.'

### Keeping a record

Some members of the *Sonderkommando* wrote down what was going on in the death camps. They hid their records in different places hoping that they would be found. This picture shows some pages of a description of the way the gas chambers of Auschwitz-Birkenau worked. They were hidden in the metal flask at the top of the picture.

## Doomed themselves

The *Sonderkommando* were kept alive for varying amounts of time in different camps – the average was about four months. During this time, some died from starvation, brutality and disease, although they had better living conditions because of the work they did. The SS regularly killed them to make a revolt less likely, leaving only enough to teach the newcomers their jobs.

# Camp discipline

The **Nazis** believed in hard work, discipline and obedience. They expected ordinary Germans to follow these rules. Prisoners in concentration camps had to be even more hard working, even more obedient. There were millions of prisoners in the camps, with not many **SS** to control them. So how did the SS control prisoners?

### Camp rules

The SS had all the advantages – they were fit, well fed and had guard dogs and weapons. Yet they were still worried about revolts in the camps. The first thing they did was to make it hard for the prisoners to get together in groups. The camp rules gave the death penalty to anyone 'discussing politics, having meetings, forming groups, loitering with others, persuading others to commit a crime, encouraging mutiny'. So prisoners had to make meeting each other accidental, and keep conversations short. However, the SS knew that it would still be possible, if difficult and dangerous, for prisoners to meet and make plans in secret.

### Prisoner against prisoner

The SS then made it difficult for prisoners to trust each other. They put prisoners in charge of other prisoners and encouraged different kinds of prisoners to hate each other. The **commandant** of Auschwitz, Rudolph Hoess, said:

> 'We encouraged various groups to see each other as enemies – we did everything we could to encourage not only the political differences, but also other antagonisms between various groups of prisoners. This made it much less likely that they would all join together against us.'

### Towers and fences

Prisoners were physically controlled and watched in the camps. Concentration camps were designed so that every part of the camp could be watched from one of the lookout towers that were built along the fence that kept everyone in. This photograph was taken standing beside one lookout tower, looking towards the next.

## Keeping moving

The SS kept everyone moving around the camps, mainly using cattle wagons like this one. This made more work for the SS – arranging the **transports**, keeping the records straight. Each time prisoners were moved they had to be taken off one set of camp lists, go through the whole arrival process again and be put on the lists in the new camp. The SS thought the work was worth it – it was another way to stop resistance groups forming. It also unsettled prisoners – all camp routines were similar, but moving prisoners meant they did not settle into a routine with familiar faces.

Of course, it was also dangerous to be an informer. It was easier for prisoners to kill an informer in their barrack or on their work gang than it was for them to kill a **kapo** or an SS guard. So informers had to rely on the SS for protection. They seldom got it – the SS could always find a new informer.

### Eyes everywhere

Prisoners were encouraged to tell the SS guards of any plots they overheard, in the same way as people outside the camp were encouraged to inform on **Jews** or **undesirables** among their neighbours. In the camps, being an informer brought real benefits. Camp informers were given more food or easier jobs, just for watching and listening. They got even better rewards if they uncovered a plot. So it was hard for prisoners to trust each other.

### Shifting people

Other things stopped people from forming settled groups. The SS deliberately changed work groups around. There was less need to move people around in the barracks – there were so many people crammed into each barrack that there was no privacy to plot against the SS. The camp population changed from other factors, too – people died in the camps all the time, either killed by the SS or from disease, starvation or overwork.

## A system of punishment

The concentration camp rules set out a clear system of punishments. They were first used in Dachau, then applied in all camps. Here are some of them:

'Punishments allowed at any time are: beatings, drilling, no mail or food, tying to stakes, reprimands and warnings.

*3 days solitary confinement for anyone who:*
Does not get up at once, or does not keep his bed or room in proper order.
Takes a second helping of food without permission, or allows the cooks to give him two helpings.

*5 days solitary confinement for anyone who:*
Sits or lies on his bed during the day without permission.

*8 days solitary confinement (and a whipping of 25 strokes before and after) for anyone who:*
Makes ironical remarks about an SS officer, or who does not show respect or in any other way does not do as he is told.
Given authority by the SS, abuses this by favouring, making false reports on or tyrannizing other prisoners.

*The following will be hanged:*
Anyone who, at any point, discusses politics; forms a political group; loiters with others; collects true or false information about the concentration camps or takes such information, buries it, passes it on to others, smuggles it out of the camp, discusses it after release or gets outside the camp by throwing it over the wall; tries, by climbing onto barrack roofs or up trees, to contact the outside world with signals, lights or so on; tries to escape, commit a crime or persuade anyone else to do so.
Anyone who attacks a guard or SS man; refuses to obey an order; encourages mutiny; leaves a marching column or place of work; shouts, agitates or makes speeches on the march or at work.'

## Bending the rules

The examples on page 30 suggest that the camp rules were clear. But, in reality, anything could be turned into a punishment, and punishment could be handed out for any reason. The rules varied from SS guard to SS guard. So, prisoners were supposed to report for **roll call** 'properly dressed'. Some SS might punish those appearing without a cap with a beating. Others would shoot the 'improperly dressed' prisoner. A standard punishment was 25 lashes of a whip or stick. However, many SS men made the prisoners count the 25 lashes themselves, in German. If the prisoner lost count they had to go back to the beginning. Many prisoners could not speak any German before they arrived in the camps.

## Punished for the 'crimes' of others

When a prisoner escaped, the SS punished the remaining prisoners. In Auschwitz I, in 1940, a prisoner was missing at noon roll call. A punishment roll call was ordered. The prisoners stood, at attention, from noon until 9 p.m. without coats, hats, jumpers or shoes. The prisoner was found dead having crawled into a doorway to shelter from the sleet. After the roll call there were 120 prisoners dead, sick or unconscious.

Once it was certain that a prisoner had escaped, the SS often executed some of the remaining prisoners. They often did this on significant days. For instance, Polish Catholics were executed on important Christian festivals, or on Polish national holidays.

### A different kind of hanging

These prisoners are being punished by being hung from posts. To the SS this was a mild punishment, so their crimes had probably been small – like not working fast enough. Although the SS saw the punishment as mild, it was torture. Prisoners hung for several hours, at the least. They lost all feeling in their hands, feet and legs. They were often beaten by guards as they hung, or worried by guard dogs, as in the picture. The picture was painted in 1946 by Wladyslaw Siwek, an ex-prisoner who, after the war, worked as an artist for the Auschwitz-Birkenau State Museum.

## Prisons

Camps were prisons in themselves. But many of the camps had prisons or punishment units attached to them. These 'Penal Companies', formed part of the camp discipline system. They were run by the 'Political' section of the camp SS (*see page 21*).

Prisoners were sent to the prison block for imprisonment in solitary confinement. People from outside the camp who tried to help prisoners, or who resisted the Nazis in other ways, were also sometimes brought to camp prisons for execution. People who tried to escape, or escaped and were re-captured, were locked up in the prison until they could be publicly executed. The ordinary cells were bad enough. Bare rooms of about 3 metres by 2 metres had between ten and twenty prisoners crowded into them with just one small high window for ventilation. Auschwitz I also had standing cells, just 90 cm by 90 cm. As many as four prisoners were crammed into one of these cells, where it was impossible to do anything but stand up. Pery Broad, an SS officer, described the standing cells after the war:

> 'Many prisoners spent terrible hours, even weeks, standing there in the dark. They could not sit down, or move about when it was cold. Breathing was almost impossible. A sentence here was almost certain death.'

### Executions

This execution wall between Block 10 (the medical experiment block) and Block 11 (the prison) in Auschwitz I is where prisoners were shot. Prisoners were also hung. One guard remembered the process: 'It went like this: one – to the stool; two – on the stool; three – read the sentence; they had to put their own head in the noose; four – stool pulled out. I pulled out one stool.'

## No escape?

The SS always made a show of re-capturing people who escaped. Sometimes they took prisoners from the nearest town jail and pretended that they were the escapees, so that prisoners thought that no one ever got away. When they did this, the SS made sure that they executed the 'escapees' quickly so no one had a chance to get a close look at them. Recaptured prisoners were marched back into camp, with everyone lined up to watch. They had to sing happy songs as they entered the camp or, as in this picture drawn by a prisoner, wear a board saying 'Here we are again!' or 'Hurrah, we're back'.

## Punishment units

The camp rules said: 'Punitive [punishment] work will be severe physical or particularly dirty work, performed under close supervision'. Prisoners in these units were not only given the hardest kind of work, they were expected to do this work while running. After their day's work they were given extra work in the evening; again, heavy manual work. Punishment units had from 150 to 600 prisoners in them at any time, and while their prisoners worked harder they were given less food than ordinary prisoners. It is not surprising that many died. Most work companies carried home several dead each day. The Penal Company took an empty cart to work and brought it back full of dead bodies – day after day.

## Women, too

Both men and women could be put into punishment units. The women's Penal Company of Auschwitz was set up in the village of Budy, about 4 kilometres (2.5 miles) from Auschwitz, in June 1942. There were 200 prisoners at first. Elfriede Runge ran the camp with 25 guards and dogs and about 20 female *kapos*. The women in this camp did mainly heavy manual work: cleaning out ponds, digging drainage ditches and repairing roads.

# Efficient camps

The **Nazis** wanted the camps to work efficiently and to pay for themselves or even make a profit. They were not to be a burden on the state – that is, cost the government anything to run. Early **SS** efficiency measures were relatively logical. As the war went on they became less and less so.

### Bureaucracy
In the Nazi system, everything had to be accounted for and everything needed the right kind of **authorization**. The **commandant** of the Auschwitz camps, Rudolf Hoess, found this affected his camps:

> 'In Berlin they were arguing over who would pay to build the camp. I had permission to build and prisons begging to send me prisoners, yet I could not get even 100 yards [91 metres] of barbed wire. There were mountains of barbed wire in the nearest Engineering Depot. But I could not touch it without authorization from Berlin. So I had to steal it, dismantling old fortifications and using all the steel, wire and other materials that I could.'

### Cheap workers
The SS used the prisoners in the camp as cheap labour. They hired them out to local businesses and, later, used them in SS-run factories, quarries and mines. The prisoners were a cheap labour force because they were not paid wages – the businesses paid the SS, not the prisoners. One of the SS officers in charge of the use of camp inmates, Karl Somer, said: 'There were about 500,000 camp prisoners working in German industry as a whole in 1941.' Prisoners were also cheap because the SS spent the absolute minimum on feeding, housing and clothing them. The SS Hygienic Institute even worked out recipes for the most economical bread and soup.

## Cheap to keep

Early prisoners in concentration camps slept on straw on the floors. Later, camp commandants introduced bunks. This was not to improve conditions for the prisoners, to give them a better night's sleep. It was because, with an average of three to each bunk, they could fit more prisoners into the same space.

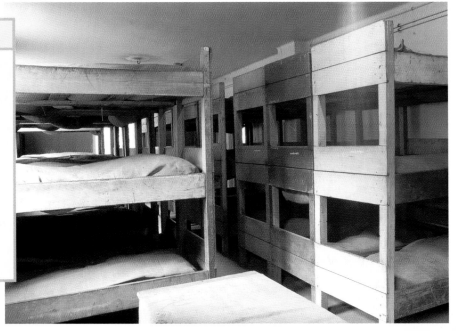

## Stolen possessions

The Nazis sold all the possessions left behind by **Jews** who emigrated, went into hiding or were taken to camps and **ghettos**. Sometimes, the possessions were given to Germans as part of the Nazi Welfare programme. They called this 'left-over Jewish effects' or 'goods taken from Jewish thieves'.

The Eigis family were Germans resettled in Poland when Germany took over Estonia. The Nazi theory was that once they took over a country, German people should be moved in to begin to make the new land part of Germany. This policy was called 'Germanization'. The Eigis family were moved to Poland and lived for a while in a transit camp in an old school, then one day:

'We were given the keys to a flat and were told how to get there. The people had left quickly, drawers were open, beds still unmade, food on the table. We found a small restaurant run by Poles and told the Nazis about it. They signed it over to us. We felt guilty. But we had to survive. We had to make a living.'

## Counting every Reichmark

The SS in Auschwitz I charged the firm I. G. Farben the correct price for transporting prisoners and guards to and from the Farben works each day from the camp. They didn't want to cheat Farben, but they didn't want the national train system to lose money either. This is how they worked it out:

'**28 Feb 1942:** There is room for 100 workers in each car. To calculate the cost of travel, the number of prisoners and supervisors [armed SS guards] transported daily is worked out. Charges are based on the price of a third class monthly ticket for up to 10 kilometres for each person [just over 0.28 **Reichmark (RM)** each]. By the end of December 1941, 158,569 people had made the journey. Cost: 45,636.80 RM.'

The SS would have already made about 600,000 RM from their charges for the workers – depending on how many guards were on the trains and how skilled the workers were. Yet they still worked out the fare to the exact 0.80 RM.

## More soldiers needed

As the war dragged on, Nazi ideas of efficiency became more extreme. More soldiers were needed and more war workers, too. So the number of SS guards had to be reduced and the number of workers increased. Also, as the Nazis moved from persecuting Jewish people to the mass murdering of them, the SS were told to find more and more efficient ways of killing people and disposing of the bodies.

In February 1942 Richard Glücks, Inspector of Concentration Camps from 1940, ordered that many fewer prisoners should clean and maintain the camp – even the sick now had to do this, to free workers for the war effort.

More soldiers were needed at the front, so Glücks wanted to find a way to keep prisoners in the camps while taking out as many of the guards as possible to send to fight. Rudolph Hoess remembered:

> 'He insisted on more and more economies, replacing men with electrified wire, dogs and minefields. Anyone who could work out a more efficient way of cutting guard numbers was promoted at once. He even imagined that dogs could be trained to circle around the prisoners, as if they were sheep, to prevent them from escaping. One sentry, with the help of several dogs, was supposed to guard 100 prisoners safely.'

## Selling tickets

The Nazis insisted that Jewish people had to have a one-way resettlement ticket for the trains that took them to the death camps. The tickets were paid for by the people themselves, the Jewish community they were taken from or, as a last resort, by the German state. Children were half price. People were even told that group bookings could be arranged. Partly, this was a Nazi trick, to reassure the Jews that they were being sent somewhere worth going to. But it was also another example of the Nazis trying to make as much money out of the

Jewish people as they could. The tickets shown here, printed in German and Greek, were bought for some of the 55,000 Greek Jews transported to Auschwitz-Birkenau.

## Hair

These rolls of cloth have been analysed by scientists, who found that they were made from human hair. Richard Glücks insisted that: 'The cut human hair in all concentration camps is to be utilized.' Men's hair was to be made into felt and yarn. Women's hair was to be made into yarn, socks for submarine crews and hair-felt stockings for workers on the German railroad. The camp commandants had to send in lists, on the fifth of every month, of the 'amounts of hair collected monthly, separated into male and female hair'. This went on at all camps.

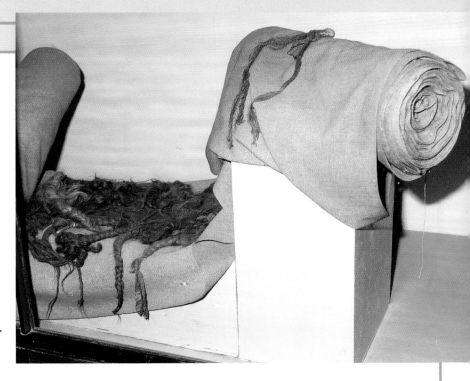

The commander of Mauthausen, Franz Ziereis, describing the camp to US soldiers after his capture at the end of the war, said: 'In almost all camps, the hair of the men, women, children was cut so it could be used for felt boots.'

### War economies

Possessions were carefully re-cycled from the moment Jews were first forced to give them up. But as the war caused hardships, so the recycling became more organized. Scissors were shipped to SS barber shops and razors and razor blades to SS canteens for resale.

Medicines and medical equipment went to army hospitals. The local SS quickly used any expensive food that was seized, while ordinary food went to feed the guards.

### The 'Final Solution'

Once the Nazis decided on the 'Final Solution' – killing all Jews – to what they called the 'Jewish Problem' they wanted to put it into practice as efficiently as possible. This meant killing more people, more quickly, for less cost and less emotional disturbance for the people who did the killing. They also wanted to make as much profit out of every single corpse as they could. So they had to not only reuse that person's possessions but also their hair, teeth and fillings – everything.

## Personal profit

When possessions were taken from Jewish people, any German money found was supposed to go straight to the SS bank in Berlin. Other money, jewellery and precious metals were sent to the Reichbank, as profit for the German state. Less valuable possessions were given out as state welfare to needy Germans. Watches, pens, clothes, shoes – everything was collected up, sorted, stored and transported from place to place. Many surviving documents show that this happened on a huge scale. In 1943 Auschwitz was shipping 20 loaded wagons of goods a day to Germany.

With all this activity, there were opportunities for stealing on every level. This was seen as stealing from the German state and was punishable by death. But many people took the risk of getting caught. A *kapo* might steal a pair of shoes, or some food. A guard might steal a watch. The higher in the SS ranks a person was, the more chance there was for making a big personal profit to hide away until after the war.

## Profit from corpses

The SS wanted to make as much money out of the Jews as they could. They worked out the most efficient way to kill as many of them as possible, as cheaply as possible. Once the Jews were dead, the SS cut off and reused any hair and took out all gold teeth and fillings. Auschwitz had a special laboratory for melting these fillings and making gold bars. They searched the bodies carefully to make sure there were no valuables hidden on them. Lastly, they got rid of them as efficiently as possible. The German firm that made the gas ovens that burned the bodies, Topf & Sons, was under pressure to keep redesigning them to take more bodies, burn them faster and use less fuel.

## Babies

The SS saw Jewish babies and young children as uneconomic and, once the Final Solution was adopted, they were sent straight to the **gas chambers**. Before this, they might have been killed or left to starve to death. This photo shows baby and toddler clothes that had not been recycled when the Russians **liberated** Auschwitz.

## Unmatched shoes

These are just a few of the shoes found at Auschwitz when it was liberated. They are not paired up and there are so many of them that it would have been impossible to match them up once they were all bundled into heaps in the barracks.

While the SS sent in reports about how many thousands of pairs of shoes were being 'stored for reuse', their system was actually falling apart. There were too many people passing through the camp for their workers to sort the goods.

## Really efficient?

Official records show how possessions were reused. But these records do not tell the whole story; they present the camp officials as more organized than they really were, especially towards the end of the war. The idea of efficiency was there, just as the Nazi leaders were still saying Germany would win the war. Reality was very different as people scrambled to save themselves. As more and more Jews arrived at Auschwitz to be gassed, there was no longer enough room in the warehouses for all their possessions. Bundles were stacked up outside, piled several feet high.

When it was clear that Soviet troops were advancing into Poland, the SS tried to destroy the evidence of the death camps and retreat. They had to leave Auschwitz in a hurry.

The Nazis only managed to partially destroy the gas chambers and the area of the camp where they stored all the belongings they had taken. What survived shows that, towards the end of the war, everything was still saved but it was not properly sorted or stored. For example, heaps of eye glasses were found, their frames rusty and their lenses broken.

# Processing arrivals at Auschwitz

All new arrivals in the camps were processed in much the same way. This is how things were done at the Auschwitz concentration camps.

## Transportation

Most prisoners arrived by train, 80 or more crammed into locked cattle wagons. The journey could take days or hours. The prisoner **transports** often had to wait while transports of soldiers and equipment used the main line. There was no air in summer and no heat in winter in the wagons. However long the journey took, the prisoners were not given any food or water. Some were given a bucket to use as a toilet – others did not even get that. People died in almost every wagon, every day. Soldiers guarded the trains to make sure that no one escaped.

## Trucks

Some prisoners arrived in lorries and trucks. Jerzy Tabeau, a Polish **political** prisoner, described his journey to Auschwitz I:

'In the yard are two small trucks. Thirty of us get into each one. The first in, stand stooped over (it is too low to stand up) next to the front wall of the truck. This first layer is about 15 people. The next in sit with their legs spread wide in front of them. This is so that one man can sit between the legs of the one behind, so 30 people are fitted into a space 2 metres by 1.5 metres. They cram us in with rifle butts, beating and shouting. In the free half of the truck stand two **SS** men with submachine guns. There are three armed motorcycle guards, too. The trucks are covered and off we go. The trip lasts one and a half hours and we are all numb at the end of it. We are beaten out of the trucks, with no allowance for the fact we find it hard to move.'

Armed SS men with attack dogs unloaded the transports. The SS deliberately made arrival noisy and confusing, then beat prisoners for not understanding and disobeying their orders. These orders were in German, not the language of the arriving prisoners. All through the process the SS beat the prisoners, cursed them and snapped out orders in German.

## Death camps

Death camps processed arrivals differently from concentration camps and labour camps. People were transported to the camps in trains. No records were made of the arrivals. Death camps only had barracks for the **Nazis** who ran them and the hundred or so *Arbeitsjuden* – 'work **Jews**' used to sort the possessions of the dead, clear out the **gas chambers** and bury or burn the bodies. Arrivals were stripped and herded straight to the gas chambers. Sometimes there were lists of the names, sometimes not. Prisoners were not given numbers and did not appear on camp records. They were in the camps for an average of two hours before they died.

## An easier journey

When smaller numbers were transported, conditions could be easier, especially if there were guards in the same van. When Hugo Gryn, who arrived in Auschwitz as a teenager, was taken from Auschwitz to the sub-camp at Lieberose guards travelled with them: 'Fifty prisoners were ordered into each wagon with three fully armed SS men. Twenty-five on one side and 25 on the other. The middle space was left for the guards.'

The train travelled all night. The guards were the last to wake in the morning. As soon as the train stopped they opened the doors to let in some air. The prisoners were then ordered out of the wagon: 'We were lined up, five by five. The guards took their places on either side, with rifles levelled horizontally, and we set off.'

### New arrivals

This painting by a prisoner, painted after the war, shows new arrivals being lined up in Auschwitz I camp. The arrivals, all men of a wide range of ages, are still in their own clothes with their possessions in cases and bundles. An officer is shouting orders at the new arrivals, while a prisoner stands at the front to show how to follow these orders properly. The officer has a whip, while the sergeant and the **kapo** at the back of the rows have sticks to beat the prisoners with.

## Worthless lives

Once prisoners were unloaded and their possessions had been taken away, the process of turning them from a person into a number began. Each stage was made as humiliating as possible, to show the prisoners how little their lives were worth. Families who had travelled together were separated into two lines: one of men and one of women with children. Arek Hersh, a young Jewish boy sent to Auschwitz from the Lodz **Ghetto**, remembers that after the groups had been split up:

'We men were marched to a small square, surrounded by electric fencing and some barracks. We were told to stop and form rows. We did so and stood there for about an hour, facing a doorway. Suddenly, the door opened and a group of naked women with their heads shaved ran out, herded by SS men with whips. They were the wives and daughters of some of the men in our group. It was degrading, sickening and shaming to watch the SS men beat these women.'

## Undressing

First, the prisoners had to take off their clothes. If they were arriving for the first time, they had to put their clothes in a paper bag, which they had to hand in for storage until their release – at least; this is what they were told. If they were being moved from one prison to another they just handed in their old prison uniform. Once they were naked, prisoners were often left for a long time, possibly hours. Sometimes they had to go through the whole process on the run. The SS were making the point that things would be done when it suited them – without any thought for the comfort of the prisoners.

### Dividing people up

These new arrivals at Auschwitz camp have been divided into two lines, male and female. Strong young men, especially those who had a useful skill, such as carpentry or metalworking, were the kind of workers the SS wanted most.

## Showers

These prisoners were photographed by the SS leaving the shower in Auschwitz-Birkenau. Hugo Gryn remembers that his arrival also included a chemical wash to prevent lice:

'The hall had a cement floor. A few inches below the ceiling were pipes with holes in them. When we were all in the showers were turned on. Within a few seconds everyone was soaking wet. I enjoyed it. I washed Dad's back and he washed mine. Suddenly the water stopped to be replaced a few seconds later with ice cold water. Then we had to go into another hall. As we went through a man ran spongy gloves all over our heads and the other places where hair grows. The liquid on the sponges was awful, for two minutes I could not get my breath back, and the places he mopped felt as if they were on fire.'

## Shaving

Prisoners were then taken to the next room, where they were shaved. Their heads were shaved, also all the other hair on their bodies. This was supposed to stop lice, which live in human hair, from spreading. But it was also used as a chance to humiliate the prisoners. A French singer, Fania Fenelon, remembers being shaved on arrival at Auschwitz:

'A young Polish woman hacked desperately at my two, thick, jet-black plaits with blunt scissors. She then attacked my head, armpits and other hair with an old rusty blade and no soap and water. She clawed and scraped. It should have hurt badly, but I don't remember – I was watching another *kapo* who had picked up my plaits and was playing with them, taunting me.'

Shaved prisoners were sent to the showers. Here again the SS played cruel games – they made the showers boiling hot or icy cold, or both, one after the other. Prisoners were not given a towel to dry with after the showers, but herded on, still wet, to the next stage of the process.

## Uniforms

Prisoners were given prison uniforms once they were showered. Most often, they were given a striped camp uniform, like the ones in this photo. However, if these had run out, they were given clothes from a previous transport of prisoners, which then had a stripe painted on. Whatever they were given to wear was usually full of lice – making the disinfection they had just gone through

pointless. Wherever possible, the clothes the prisoners were given did not fit – this was to make the prisoners look ridiculous. Mostly they were issued wooden clogs to wear on their feet, outsized if possible. This meant they found it harder to walk and keep in step, giving the SS another opportunity to punish them.

## Registration

The prisoners also had to be registered. A *kapo* wrote down their details on a form – name, address, nationality, relatives, job and so on. The forms were kept by the Political division of the camp SS, which made ten to twenty copies of lists of the prisoners, which they sent to different offices in the camp and in Berlin.

Tadeusz Sobolewicz, a Polish 'political' prisoner who spoke German, had to register those Jews at Auschwitz-Birkenau who did not go straight to the gas chambers:

'The SS man handed out thick wads of forms. He spent a long time explaining the information we had to get from the prisoners and where to write it down. We were warned: "You're only allowed to ask questions. Fill in the forms, don't talk, tell them nothing." The first transport was from Holland. There was a stream of men coming to our tables. I had to write almost without pause. "Where and when were you born? Name? Where did you live? Where do you want your letters sent?" It was hard work and I knew it wasn't needed, any of this information.'

## Just a number

Once prisoners were registered, they were given a number. In all the camps, prisoners were given a number to sew on to their clothing. In some camps they were also given a number to wear around their wrists. From that point on, they were never spoken to by name, just by number.

Sometimes it could be useful not being seen as a person. Tadeusz Sobolewicz was caught sleeping in the daytime by the SS and was told to report to the Penal Company. Most people sent to this punishment unit died within days. Tadeusz's friends managed to swap his uniform with the uniform of a dead prisoner. He lived pretending to be the dead prisoner for a few days. His friends, who knew a clerk in the offices, got the clerk to switch numbers to make it seem that the dead man, not Tadeusz, had been sent to the Penal Company. This would not have been possible if the SS had looked on their prisoners as people, not numbers.

## Tattoos

In Auschwitz, from 1942 onwards, prisoners also had their number tattooed onto their arm. Auschwitz was the only camp to tattoo prisoners. This was because there were so many prisoners and the death rate was so high – sometimes several hundred a day. Tattooing made it easier for the SS to keep track of all the prisoners.

### Prisoner photographs

Most death camps simply made lists of the prisoners. In Auschwitz they also photographed most of their early prisoners. Some of the photos, like this set, survived and are in Auschwitz I, which is now a state museum. Most Jews were not photographed and, as the war went on, supplies of photographic equipment ran out. Photographing stopped in 1943. These photos show prisoner

number 26947. Her name was Katarzyna Kwoka and she was arrested as a political prisoner. She was brought to Auschwitz I on 13 December 1942, from Zamosc, Poland. She died on 6 February 1943.

## Obedience

One of the most important lessons for **quarantine** prisoners was to obey any orders at once. Prisoners might have a day-long **roll call** or have to learn German marching songs or play leap-frog all day or do various exercises. Sometimes they spent the entire day taking their caps off and putting them on. Beatings were handed out all through the day. Tadeusz Sobolewicz remembers his first day in quarantine:

'The last of the work squads marched out through the main gate, while the rest went about their work in the camp. We still stood there, trying to keep warm. Then the SS men and the ***blockältesters*** came out and announced we had not taken our caps off the right way during roll call. So we had to lie on the ground, face down. As soon as we had done that we had to get up again. And so on: "Get up! Lie down! Get up! Lie down!" over and over. The SS men and the **prisoner functionaries** were laughing together at this. But it was only the beginning. "Now, pay attention," said the *blockältester*. Now we had to hold our caps in our right hands and slap them against our right thighs, all at the same time. Of course, we couldn't. Those who had been too slow were pulled out of line, lined up against the wall and questioned. The Jews and priest among them were repeatedly punched in the face, so that their heads then bounced off the wall. This sort of thing went on all day.'

### Surviving quarantine

This photo shows the quarantine camp at Mauthausen after **liberation**. In the background you can see the fence that separates the quarantine area from the rest of the camp.

## Put to work

These prisoners in Neuengamme labour camp have been taken from quarantine into the main camp and put to work.

## Learning the routine

Quarantine also got prisoners used to the camp routine. They got up at about 4 a.m. They had to make their beds neatly, use the toilets, wash and dress as quickly as possible. They were then given breakfast and were rushed out to roll call. All through this, they had to move quickly, do things 'properly' and obey orders in German. Any mistake, however small, meant a beating. For roll call they lined up in rows of ten as it made them easier to count. There was a roll call morning and evening. After the evening roll call the prisoners lined up for an evening meal. By 9 p.m. they were in their barracks and not allowed out until morning.

## Part of the camp

Once quarantine was over, the prisoners became part of the camp. They were moved out of the quarantine barracks to make room for newcomers, and into ordinary barracks. Here they followed the same getting up routines they had been taught, but they were put into work groups and worked from 6 a.m. to 5 p.m. with a half-hour meal break. This was the official work time. Many prisoners worked for far longer.

Leon Greeman, an English Jew, was transferred to Auschwitz I and worked for a while at unloading bricks: 'You had four, six or eight bricks loaded onto your shoulders and had to walk to a heap and unload them. The tops of my fingers were soon scraped raw.'

# The main camps

This map and list are of the main camps in Greater Germany, a term used by the Nazis that included Germany, Austria, Czechoslovakia and parts of Poland. They do not include all sub-camps, or any prisoner-of-war camps or holding camps. Nor do they mention camps elsewhere in occupied Europe (for instance there was a camp as far away as Alderney in the Channel Islands).

## Camps in Greater Germany

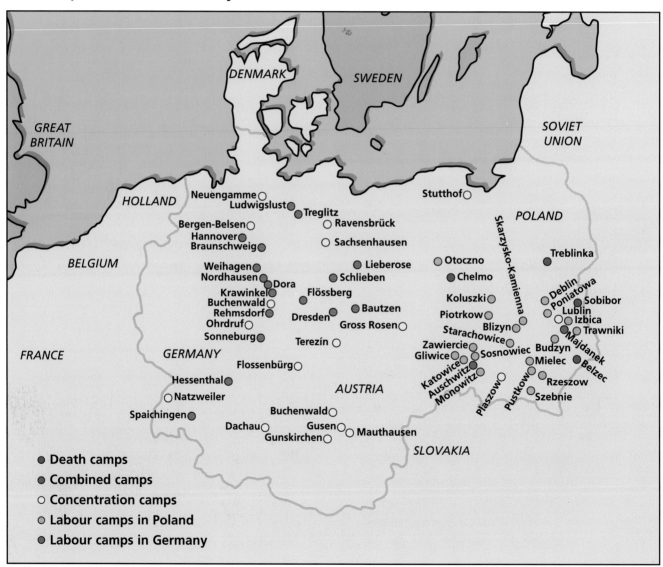

- ● Death camps
- ● Combined camps
- ○ Concentration camps
- ◐ Labour camps in Poland
- ● Labour camps in Germany

## Death camps
Belzec
Chelmno
Sobibor
Treblinka

## Combined camps
Auschwitz-Birkenau
Majdanek

## Concentration camps
Bergen-Belsen
Buchenwald
Dachau
Flossenbürg
Gross Rosen
Gunskirchen
Gusen
Lublin
Mauthausen
Natzweiler
Neuengamme
Novaky
Sachsenhausen
  [Oranienburg]
Plaszow
Ravensbrück
Stutthof
Terezín [Theresienstadt]

## Labour camps and sub-camps in Poland
Blizyn
Bochnia
Budzyn
Czestochowa
Deblin
Gliwice
Izbica
Katowice
Koluszki
Mielec
Monowitz
Otoczno
Piotrkow
Poniatowa
Pustkow
Rzeszow
Skarzysko-Kamienna
Sosnowiec
Szebnie
Trawniki
Zawiercie

## Labour camps in Germany
Bautzen
Braunschweig
Dora
Dresden
Flossberg
Hannover
Hessenthal
Krawinkel
Lieberose
Ludwigslust
Nordhausen
Rehmsdorf
Schlieben
Sonneberg
Spaichingen
Treglitz
Wiehagen

### Majdanek

An aerial view of Majdanek concentration and death camp taken by the Allies during the war.

# Timeline

**1933**

| | |
|---|---|
| **30 January** | The **Nazi** Party comes to power in Germany. Adolf Hitler, their leader, is elected Chancellor. |
| **27 February** | Fire breaks out at the Reichstag, the German parliament |
| **28 February** | Hindenburg's decree 'For the Protection of the People and the State', allows for the creation of concentration camps. The Nazis persuaded Hindenburg to pass the decree to fight what they call the '**Communist** threat' after the fire at the Reichstag. |
| **17 March** | **SS** set up, as Hitler's bodyguard |
| **21 March** | Dachau, the first Nazi concentration camp, set up. Concentration camps and labour camps set up steadily after this. |
| **2 May** | Trade unions banned in Germany |
| **14 July** | Political parties other than the Nazi Party banned in Germany |

**1934**

| | |
|---|---|
| **20 July** | SS becomes the most important of Hitler's 'private armies' |
| **2 August** | Hitler makes himself *Führer*, sole leader of Germany |

**1936**

| | |
|---|---|
| **29 March** | SS grows to 3500 men |
| **17 June** | Himmler put in charge of all police departments |

**1937**

| | |
|---|---|
| **16 July** | Buchenwald concentration camp set up |

**1938**

| | |
|---|---|
| **13 March** | German army marches into Austria. The Austrians vote to become part of Germany. |
| **8 August** | Mauthausen concentration camp set up |
| **9 November** | *Kristallnacht*: Nazi-led violence against **Jewish** people, in which synagogues burned, shops and homes looted |

**1939**

| | |
|---|---|
| **1 September** | Germany invades Poland. Nazis begin to pass laws against Polish Jews restricting the work they can do, as in Germany in 1933–6. |
| **3 September** | Britain and France declare war on Germany |
| **17 September** | Soviet Union invades Poland from the east |
| **28 September** | Germany and the Soviet Union split Poland up between them |

**1940**

| | |
|---|---|
| **12 February** | First German Jews forced into **ghettos** in Poland |
| **9 April** | Germany invades Denmark and Norway |
| **27 April** | Himmler builds a camp at Auschwitz |
| **30 April** | A large ghetto is set up in the Polish city of Lodz. All Jews from the city and the surrounding area are sent there. More ghettos are planned in other Polish cities for Polish Jews, and then for Jews from other lands controlled by Germany. |
| **10 May** | Germany invades Belgium, France, Luxembourg and the Netherlands. Defeat of France. |

## 1941

| | |
|---|---|
| **6 April** | Germany invades Yugoslavia and Greece |
| **22 June** | Germany invades the Soviet Union; mass executions of Jews as the German army moves through the Soviet Union |
| **25 June** | Finland declares war on Russia and so becomes an ally of Germany |
| **1 September** | All German Jews over the age of six have to wear a yellow Star of David with '*Jude*' in black on it |
| **September** | Mass gassings at Auschwitz begin with Soviet prisoners-of-war. They then focus on Jews and become more regular from January 1942. |
| **16 October** | Mass deportation of German Jews to Poland begins |
| **28 October** | 10,000 Jews selected and killed at Kovno Ghetto, Lithuania |
| **7 December** | Japan bombs the US fleet at Pearl Harbor, bringing the USA into the war |
| **8 December** | First gassing of Jews, at Chelmno |
| **11 December** | Germany declares war on USA |

## 1942

| | |
|---|---|
| **20 January** | Wannsee Conference; outlines the 'Final Solution' to what the Nazis call the 'Jewish Problem' |
| **1 March** | First deportation of Jews from lands controlled by the Nazis to Sobibor death camp |
| **17 March** | First deportation of Jews to Belzec death camp |
| **26 March** | First deportations to Auschwitz-Birkenau and Majdanek death camps |
| **27 March** | First deportation of French Jews to Auschwitz |
| **15 July** | First deportation of Dutch Jews to Auschwitz |
| **22 July** | Daily deportations to Treblinka from the Warsaw Ghetto begin |
| **4 October** | Himmler orders that all Jews in concentration camps are to be sent to Auschwitz-Birkenau to be killed |

## 1943

| | |
|---|---|
| **11 June** | Himmler orders all ghettos closed and their inhabitants killed |

## 1944

| | |
|---|---|
| **23 March** | Deportation of Jews from Greece (occupied by the Germans) begins |
| **7 April** | Two Jews escape from Auschwitz and send news of the camp out of occupied Europe to the **Allies**. Information about the Holocaust cannot now be ignored. |
| **15 May** | Mass deportation and gassing of Hungarian Jews begins |
| **From June** | Death marches from camps in the east. Prisoners are marched westward, in front of advancing Soviet troops. |
| **6 June** | Allied troops land in Normandy, France |

## 1945

| | |
|---|---|
| **17 January** | Final death march from Auschwitz-Birkenau |
| **27 January** | Soviet troops reach Auschwitz |
| **11 April** | US troops reach Buchenwald |
| **15 April** | British troops reach Belsen |
| **29 April** | US troops reach Dachau |
| **30 April** | Hitler commits suicide in Berlin, as the city is occupied by Soviet troops |
| **5 May** | US troops reach Mauthausen |
| **7 May** | Germany surrenders |
| **20 November** | Nuremberg trials of Nazi war criminals begin. First war criminals executed in October 1946. |

# Glossary

**Allies** used to mean the various countries that fought against Nazi Germany in the Second World War

**Aryan** race of people invented by the Nazis to mean people with northern European ancestors. Aryans do not have any ancestors from so-called inferior races, such as Poles, Slavs or Jews. They were usually blonde, blue-eyed and sturdy.

**asocial** the Nazis called people this if they did not support the Nazi state. Asocials could be alcoholics, people who would not work, homosexuals or members of a religious group whose beliefs might make them oppose the Nazis.

**authorization** written permission to do something from someone in power

**blockältester** prisoner put in charge of a barracks (women were called *blockälteste*)

**cholera** disease that causes vomiting, diarrhoea and can be fatal. It is caused by dirty conditions and spread by water polluted with sewage.

**citizen** person who belongs to a country and who has rights in that country (such as protection by the law) and duties to that country (such as paying taxes)

**commandant** person in charge of a camp

**Communist** person who believes that a country should be governed by the people of that country for the good of everyone in it. Communists believe private property is wrong – from owning a home to running a business. The state should own everything and run everything, giving the people the things they need in return.

**crematorium** place with special ovens for burning bodies

**Einsatzkommando** 'killing squad' sent to the Soviet Union with the invading German army. These squads had the job of rounding up and killing as many Jewish people, Slavs and other people the Nazis saw as sub-human, as possible.

**frostbite** infection of the skin caused by extreme cold. Untreated frostbite can cause gangrene, which makes the affected part of the body rot away.

**gas chambers** large rooms, often disguised as showers, that the Nazis filled with people. When the rooms were full the Nazis pumped gas into them, to kill the people inside.

**Gestapo** secret police set up by the Nazis in 1933

**ghetto** area of a town or city, walled or fenced off from the rest of the city, where Jewish people were forced to live.

**Holocaust** in ancient times 'an offering to the gods that was completely burnt away'. By medieval times it meant 'a huge destruction or sacrifice'. It is now mostly used to describe the Nazis' attempt to kill all the Jewish people in Europe.

**Jehovah's Witnesses** religious group that was especially persecuted by the Nazis because members refused to swear an oath of loyalty to Hitler

**Jews (Jewish)** people who follow Judaism. The Nazis also called people Jews if they had Jewish ancestors, even if they had changed their faith.

*Judenfrei* 'Jew Free' – a place with no Jewish people living there

*kapo* prisoner who is put in charge of other prisoners when they are working, to make sure that they work hard

**liberated** the freeing of a place, especially a camp from the control of the SS. Camps were liberated by Allied and Russian soldiers.

**Nazi** member of the Nazi Party. Nazi is short for *Nationalsozialistische Deutsche Arbeiterpartei*: the National Socialist German Workers' Party.

**political** person arrested for opposing Nazi idea or actions.

**propaganda** information and ideas given to people in a way that will make them accept those ideas

**protective custody** arrest under the law 'For the Protection of the People and the State', passed in February 1933, which allowed the German police to arrest people for as long as they like without bringing them to trial

**quarantine** medical word meaning keeping people who might be carrying a disease away from other people, in case they spread that disease. Used by the Nazis to talk about the first few days or weeks people spent in a new camp. The Nazis said the quarantine was medical, but it was really to terrorize the prisoners into obedience.

**race** group of people with the same ancestors

**Reich/Third Reich** empire – the Nazis saw their rule as the third German empire, with Hitler as the emperor, or *Führer*.

**Reichmark (RM)** German money under the Nazis

**roll call** the counting of all the prisoners in a camp. Camps usually had roll call morning and evening.

**SS** short for *Schutzstaffel* – security staff. The SS began as Hitler's personal guard. Later, they ran the camps. All the SS swore loyalty to Hitler, not Germany.

**selection** used to refer to the SS process in the camps of choosing which people to kill

**transport** used to refer to a load of people being sent to the camps

**typhus** disease caused by dirty conditions and spread by polluted water, usually polluted with sewage. Typhus causes high temperatures, rashes, vomiting and diarrhoea. It can be fatal.

**undesirables** word used by the Nazis to mean any person that they did not approve of because of their political beliefs, their race, their religion or their behaviour

# Further reading

*Auschwitz*, Jane Shuter  (Heinemann Library, 1999)
*Diary of a Young Girl*, Anne Frank (Penguin, 1997)
*Ten Thousand Children: True stories Told by Children Who Escaped the Holocaust on the Kindertransport*, Anne L Fox and Eva Abraham-Podietz (Behrman House, 1997)
*The Beautiful Days of My Youth*, Ana Novac (Henry Holt, 1992)
*The Cap, or The Price of a Life*, Roman Frisker (Weidenfeld & Nicolson, 1999)
*The Past is Myself*, Christabel Bielenberg (Chatto and Windus, 1984)
*Tomi, a Childhood under the Nazis*, Tomi Ungerer (Roberts Rinehart, 1998)

## Sources

The author and Publishers gratefully acknowledge the publications from which written sources in the book are drawn. In some cases the wording or sentence structure has been simplified to make the material appropriate for a school readership.

*'The Nazi State: Machine or Morass'*, in *History Today*, (History Today Ltd, 1986) pp. 9, 32
*Auschwitz 1270 to the Present*, Robert Jan de Pelt and Deborah Dwork (Yale University Press, 1996) pp. 7, 13
*Auschwitz Nazi Death Camp* (Auschwitz-Birkenau State Museum, 1996) pp. 20, 40
*But I Survived*, Tadeusz Sobolewicz, translated by Witold Zbirohowski-Koscia (Oswiecim: Auschwitz-Birkenau State Museum, 1998) pp. 25, 44, 46
*Chasing Shadows*, Hugo Gryn (Viking, 2000) pp. 25, 26, 41, 43
*KL Auschwitz seen by the SS*, (Auschwitz Birkenau State Museum, 1997) pp. 10, 14, 16, 21–2, 27–8, 32, 34, 36
*Nazism, 1919-1945*, J. Noakes and G Pridham (University of Exeter Press, 1991) pp. 4, 9, 15, 30, 37
*Planet Dora*, Yves Beon (Westview, 1997) pp. 20, 24
*The Boys*, Martin Gilbert (Weidenfeld and Nicholson, 1996) p. 42
*The Good Old Days: The Holocaust as Seen by its Perpetrators and Bystanders*, edited by Ernst Klee, Willi Dressen and Volker Riess (Konecky and Konecky, 1991) pp. 19, 23, 24, 32
*The Holocaust for Beginners*, Haim Bresheeth, Stuart Hood and Litza Jansz (Icon books, 1994) p. 19
*The Nazis, a Warning from History*, Laurence Rees (BBC Books, 1997) p. 35

# Places of interest and websites

## Museums and exhibitions

Imperial War Museum
Lambeth Road, London SE16 6HZ
Tel: 020 7416 5320
Website: *http://www.iwm.org.uk*
The Imperial War Museum in London now has a permanent Holocaust exhibition.

London Jewish Museum
Raymond Burton House, 129-131 Albert Street, London NW1 7NB
Tel: 020 7284 1997
Website: *http://www.jewishmuseum.org.uk*
Or:
The Sternberg Centre, 80 East End Road, London N3 2SY
Tel: 020 8349 1143
The London Jewish Museum regularly features exhibitions and talks about the Holocaust.

Sydney Jewish Museum
146 Darlinghurst Road, Darlinghurst, NSW 2010
Tel: (02) 9360 7999
Website: *www.join.org.au/sydjmus/*
The Sydney Jewish Museum contains a permanent Holocaust exhibition, using survivors of the Holocaust as guides.

## Websites

Before consulting any websites you need to know:

1 Almost all Holocaust websites have been designed for adult users. They can contain horrifying and upsetting information and pictures.
2 Some people wish to minimize the Holocaust, or even deny that it happened at all. Some of their websites pretend to be delivering unbiased facts and information. To be sure of getting accurate information it is always better to use an officially recognized site such as the ones listed below.

*www.ushmm.org*
This is the US Holocaust Memorial Museum site.

*www.iwm.org.uk*
The Imperial War Museum site. You can access Holocaust material from the main page.

*www.holocaust-history.org*
This is the Holocaust History Project site.

*www.auschwitz.dk*
The Holocaust: Crimes, Heroes and Villains site.

*http://motlc.wiesenthal.com*
The Museum of Tolerance's Multimedia Learning Centre site.

# Index